Winter
on the farm

by Jillian Powell

HODDER
Wayland

an imprint of Hodder Children's Books

Titles in the series

Summer on the farm
Autumn on the farm
Winter on the farm
Spring on the farm

Picture Acknowledgements
The publishers would like to thank the following for allowing their photographs to be reproduced in this book:
Agripicture/Peter Dean title page, 13, 23 (top), 25, 28 both, 29; J Allan Cash Ltd 27 top; Bruce Coleman Ltd 17 (George McCarthy); Sylvia Cordaiy Photo Library 26 (Helen Wilcocks); Frank Lane Picture Agency front cover (M.J Thomas), 7, 27 bottom (M.J Thomas), 12 (A.J Roberts), 22 (E.& D Hosking); Natural History Photographic Agency 4, 9 bottom (David Woodfall), 5 bottom (G.I Bernard), 6 (E.A Janes), 14 both (Laurie Campbell); Oxford Scientific Films (Bridget Wheeler/Survival Anglia), 11 (G.A Maclean), 18 top (Breck Kent), 20 (G.I Bernard), 21 (Martyn Chillmaid), 23 bottom (Martin Wendler/Okapia); STB/Still Moving 15; Tony Stone Worldwide 8, 9 top (Annette Soumillard), 16 (Oliver Benn); Wayland Picture Library back cover, 5 top, 18 bottom, 19, 24, 30, 31.

Series editors: Francesca Motisi and Sarah Doughty
Book editor: Joan Walters
Series and book designer: Jean Wheeler

First published in Great Britain in 1996
by Wayland (Publishers) Ltd
This edition printed in 2001 by Hodder Wayland,
an imprint of Hodder Children's Books

British Library Cataloguing in Publication Data

Powell, Jillian
Winter on the Farm
1. Agriculture – Juvenile literature 2. Winter – Juvenile literature
I. Title

ISBN 0-7502-3425-3

Typeset by Jean Wheeler
Printed and bound in Hong Kong

Contents

Introduction

In winter, the weather becomes colder. The nights may be frosty and it may be cold enough to snow. Some animals come indoors, although sheep can stay outside because of their long, woolly coats. The farmer must see that the sheep have enough to eat and do not become stuck in the snow.

Cattle are brought into covered yards or sheds to keep them warm and dry. Other animals that come indoors in winter are deer and goats.

The farmer has to keep a watch around the farm. There may be winter jobs to be done, such as mending buildings and fences.

The cereal farm

The ground may be hard and icy in winter but some crops are strong enough to grow even through the winter months.

Here a farmer sprays chemicals on to a crop of winter barley. This helps to keep the plants healthy. The tractor pulls the sprayer which spreads the chemicals on to the fields.

Plants also need food to grow
well. Many farmers put
food back into the earth by
spreading animal manure over
the fields, using a machine
called a muck spreader.
Crops can also be sprayed with
plant foods called fertilizers.

Tunnels and glasshouses

Many plants cannot grow outside in winter because it is too cold and frosty.

Some farmers grow their crops in glasshouses.

Others grow their crops in polytunnels made of strong, see-through polythene.

Vegetables, such as tomatoes and lettuces, are grown in tunnels and glasshouses. Flowers are also grown.

Growing plants indoors stops the wind, snow and frost from spoiling the plants. Being under cover, the area traps all the warmth of the sun.

The fruit farm

In winter, many trees lose their leaves and their branches are bare.

Winter is the time to plant new trees, which come from a nursery. The farmworkers plant out the trees in rows. Each tree is tied to a strong post which helps it to grow straight. In two years' time the trees will be big enough to grow fruit.

The older trees have their branches cut back in winter. This is called pruning. It stops the trees becoming too big and it helps them grow more fruit next year.

Cattle in winter

In winter, fields become muddy or snowy and there is not enough fresh grass for cattle to eat.

As the weather gets colder, the farmer brings the cattle indoors to cattle yards or sheds. Here, they can stay warm and dry for the winter. The farmer gives the cattle straw to sleep on and feeds them on hay and silage.

When the sheds are cleaned out the manure is stored in a pit.

The cattle will live outside again when the grass begins to grow in the spring.

The deer farm

Some farmers keep deer
for their meat, which is
called venison.

Deer graze on grass
and heather for most
of the year. In winter
the farmer may feed the
deer on hay or silage, and
perhaps some nuts.

If the weather becomes very cold, wet or snowy in winter, deer must find somewhere to shelter.

Sometimes the farmer brings the deer indoors where they will be fed and kept warm and dry.

The young deer calves which were born in the spring are now checked and weighed to make sure they are healthy.

The sheep farm

Sheep can stay outdoors through the winter where they feed on short grass. There are strong breeds of sheep, such as Scottish Blackface, which can live high in the hills.

When snow covers the ground, the farmer uses a tractor to take bales of hay or silage out for the sheep to eat.

The female sheep are called ewes.
Some ewes have their lambs in the
winter months.

The farmer brings the ewes into lambing
sheds. Lambs which are born outdoors in
winter could die in cold, snowy weather.
Indoors, the ewes stay warm and dry and
the farmer can help them give birth to
their lambs.

The fish farm

Winter is the time when fish eggs hatch into tiny fish called fish fry. They are given special food with lots of protein in it to help them grow quickly.

When they are bigger, they are moved into larger tanks of water and given more food.

Farmworkers catch the fish in
big nets. They carry them in
tanks of water on the back of
a trailer to the bigger ponds.

Indoor and outdoor farming

Animals can live outdoors in winter as long as they have shelters to sleep in at night. Keeping animals outdoors where they are free to walk about is called free-range farming.

The hen house is home to these free-range hens.

Hens like to scratch about for food outside but the farmer also brings them extra food.

These pigs are free to find food in the fields but they are also given pellets of food. The pellets are scattered about the fields or put in a feeding trough.

Pigs can shelter in pig huts if the weather is too cold or wet.

Some farmers keep their pigs or hens indoors all year round. The heating and lighting stay the same whether it is winter or summer.

Indoor pigs live in big sheds. It is warm and light inside so the female pigs give birth to piglets even in winter. The piglets grow quickly.

Young chickens that are reared for meat are kept indoors in big, warm barns with straw on the floor. They never go outside, even in spring or summer.

Egg-laying hens may be kept in rows of cages. The farmer uses electric lighting so it is like springtime to the hens. This makes them go on laying eggs in the winter.

Free-range hens stop laying eggs in the winter months. When the days become longer in the spring, free-range hens start laying again.

A visit from the vet

Farmers must check their animals in the winter to make sure they are all well. If an animal is sick, the farmer will call the vet.

The vet looks at the animals to find out what is wrong and sometimes gives the animal medicine.

Winter is the time for the farmer to plan ahead so that cows will have calves next autumn. The most healthy cows are left with a bull like this one, to be mated. They will give birth to calves in about eight months' time.

Winter jobs around the farm

In winter, there are lots of jobs to do around the farm. Winter is the time to clear any leaves and twigs from the ditches around the farm fields.

Ditches let the rain run away from the fields and stop them getting muddy. Crops cannot grow in the fields if they are too wet or muddy.

The farmer uses a digger to clear the ditches and dig out new ones.

The farmer may need to mend old farm buildings and walls or build new ones. Walls and fences are important for keeping farm animals in the fields.

Planning ahead

In the winter months, the farmer will make sure that all the farm machinery is working properly.

The machines are cleaned and repaired so they are ready to use in the spring.

The days are short in winter so the farmer may spend the long, dark evenings planning ahead for next year's farming.

Winter is the time to decide which crops
to grow and which fields to plant them in.

The computer keeps all the information
about the farm crops and animals.
It can tell the farmer how much milk
each cow makes every day, and how well
each crop grew in the summer months.

The farming year calendar

Spring

Sowing crops for summer and autumn harvest

Harvesting vegetables grown through the winter

Fertilizing and spraying crops against weeds and diseases

Lambing

Putting animals out to graze

Silage making

Summer

Harvesting vegetables and soft fruits

Watering crops

Haymaking

Silage making

Sheep shearing and sheep dipping

Harvesting crops like wheat and barley

Autumn

Ploughing fields after
 harvest
Sowing winter wheat
 and barley
Harvesting fruits such as
 apples and pears
Harvesting potatoes and
 sugar beet
Autumn calving
Hedge trimming

Winter

Clearing and draining
 ditches
Pruning fruit trees
Housing animals
Early indoor lambing
Fertilizing crops
Repairing farm
 buildings, fences
 and machinery

Glossary

Chemicals Powders or sprays made up by scientists.

Fertilizer Special plant food sprayed on to fields to help crops grow.

Hay Grass which has been dried in the sun.

Manure Animal dung, such as cowpats, which is spread on to fields to help crops grow.

Mated When a male and female animal have joined together to produce young.

Nursery A sort of garden centre where farmers can buy young plants and trees.

Polythene Sheets of strong, see-through plastic.

Protein A part of food that helps with growth and repair.

Silage Grass that has been cut and wrapped in black plastic to keep it juicy.

Vet A short word for veterinary surgeon, meaning animal doctor.

Books to read

Farming, Sue Hadden (Wayland, 1991)

Farming, Ruth Thomson (Watts, 1994)

Let's Visit a Farm series, Sarah Doughty and Diana Bentley (Wayland, 1989-90)

Index